My Perfect Emotionless World

A Memoir of My Life Before I Knew I was on the Spectrum

Anna Jorgensen

ARI Press

SAN FRANCISCO

Editor. Anonymous.

Cover Art: Hope Coleman Designs

DISCLAIMER: This is a memoir that reflects the author's personal recollections of experiences and events that may or may not be how others remember them. In order to maintain anonymity, many names of individuals and places have been changed.

ISBN 978-0-578-78398-7 (Paperback)

Second Edition 2020

To my family

Preface

I always knew I was different. When I was little, my mom told me I had a "special quality." She said that someday I would be really successful and that my special quality would lead me to do great things…"but" she would say, "now is not the time to use your special quality. You need to learn to tuck it into your back pocket, because other people don't understand." Over the years, I learned that my special quality liked to come out at the most inopportune times and it was my job to keep it at bay.

The DSM-5 calls it an Autism Spectrum Disorder. To me, it's when you're normal enough that people expect the same of you as they do everyone else, but you are also autistic enough that you don't always meet those expectations. From the day you are born, you know there's something different about you, but you can't quite put your finger on it. And, once you learn to navigate through a world where most people think in a much different way than you do, you become a chameleon. You learn the unwritten social rules of society, and try to follow them to blend in with the majority as best you can.

I am somewhere on the autism spectrum, and I have been since I was born. However, I didn't know this until I was formally diagnosed at 22 years old. The symptoms have been present my whole life, but, as I grew up, I learned how to better manage my environment and interactions with others, making it harder for my intellectual differences and social faux pas to be noticed.

My coming of age memoir is one of hardship, success, discrimination, inclusion, sadness, and love. It's the story of a girl who was smart, caring, athletic, and passionate, but struggled internally to fit in and find her place among her peers. In this story, I will take you directly into my own world so that you can experience my undiagnosed autism much like I did.

Part 1

Challenges at School

1

Anna

By my senior year of high school, I had completely given up on everything. The pain and sadness in my heart was too much to handle. On an almost daily basis, I would tell my parents that I hated Morgan High and wanted to quit school. My mother always responded the same way. She would say: "Anna, can't you see it, there's a light at the end of the tunnel. You're almost done." But I could never see it. There was no light.

It's strange to look back and remember what my life used to be like during high school. So many things have changed since then, and I think I've finally accepted my life now as my new reality. After struggling to understand why my life was suddenly so different, I was told that: "the more good things that happen to you where other people show you they care, the more you're going to believe that there is nothing wrong with you." I was also told that: "As more time passes, what happened to you will seem smaller and it won't affect you as much." It's true. As the distance becomes greater, the things that hurt you the most seem smaller, and you become less afraid that they'll happen again.

As I went through my college years, it was really hard for me to trust people, because I was confused. Confused about why I suddenly had all of these amazing people surrounding me and filling my days with laughter, fun, and joy. These are the people I now call my friends. In the beginning it was weird for me to think: *Anna has friends? Anna has people who text her, who sit with her at meals? Who want to hang out and spend time with her? And it's not just one person? It's many?* After being alone at school for so long, I never thought I'd be able to say that I have a friend. Someone to eat with and talk to. After being treated a certain way for many years, I came to believe that there was something wrong with me and that I deserved to be treated like such was true. I believed I was unworthy of friendship, because I simply wasn't good enough.

No matter how hard I tried to be perfect, I just wasn't good enough for everybody else.

2

The Beginning

In the spring of my 8th grade year, I had been accepted to the Anna Feld School. I had been so intrigued by the prestigious high school on my shadow visit. It was a private college preparatory also known as one of the Bay Area "feeder" schools to a coveted Ivy League college education. At the time, I had really high expectations for myself, so I left my group of middle school friends to attend this private high school that was a half hour from my hometown in the heart and center of Oakland, CA.

I was really excited to get there, get involved, and make new friends. However, within the first couple of weeks, it was apparent that making new friends was going to be a challenge.

On the second week of school, they had the annual "Club Day." I decided to join the Asia Club. I chose to join the Asia club because I had recently taken a trip to India with my grandparents and was mildly obsessed with traveling to that part of the world. Upon my arrival to the first Asia club meeting, I noticed that everyone was eating Asian food. I was eager to fit in and asked one of the club leaders if we were supposed to bring Asian food to eat at lunch during the club meeting days. The club leader replied that it wasn't required, but that some of the students liked to for fun. Little did I know, another girl in the room had taken offense to what I had said. She was an athletic, half Asian girl who proceeded to tell me that my question about food was racist. She went behind my back and the next day told our Asian English teacher that I was making racist comments to her. The teacher pulled me aside after class the next day and took me into another building where she sat me down with another Asian English teacher. Together, they blatantly accused me of being racist and making racist comments. Of course, I was taken by surprise and devastated at the mere thought of being accused of making racially inappropriate comments to my peers. I hated getting in trouble, and I left school in tears. When I returned home, my mother sent an angry email to my

English teacher, who ended up apologizing to me later that week for mishandling the situation.

Even though it was evident to me that the school year was off to a rough start, I was still determined to find my path at this prestigious high school. Everyday, I smiled at people and said hi to them on my way to classes. I was trying my best to appear friendly and make new friends. It was weird to me that while some of my peers knew my name and smiled back, no one seemed to want to be my friend. I quickly resorted to eating lunch by myself, usually alone and far away from everyone else, either up in the gardens or in the library where I thought no one would notice me. I thought that if I stayed in the library it looked like I was doing homework. I remember feeling so alone and isolated. Class became difficult for me as well. The classes at Anna Feld were heavily discussion based, which made it hard for me to follow along. I had trouble finding times to break into the group discussions and participate, so I kept to myself and tried to listen as best as I could.

Looking back now, it's easy for me to see that I simply didn't fit in there. I definitely did not fit the mold of a typical Anna Feld student. So I was labeled very quickly. Most of the student body was from the

Oakland/Berkeley area and appeared to me to place their values on diversity, our new President, Barack Obama, and really anything democratic or liberal. I try to stay away from politics, but I think that the way I appeared came off wrong. I was from a town on the other side of the tunnel in one of the wealthiest suburbs outside of San Francisco. During that year, I frequently heard students talking negatively about people from my hometown. They sometimes referred to us as "Tunnel Rats" or in other words the rich kids who come through the tunnel occasionally to hang out on College Avenue in Berkeley. The big thing they said about kids from my hometown was that they thought we could "afford" to buy alcohol or that our parents bought it for us all of the time and then threw us fancy parties with bouncers so that we could get drunk. I can see where this view might have come from, but regardless of its validity, many of the students at Anna Feld seemed to look down upon "tunnel rats" and their "way of life." I am from the other side of the tunnel, so I definitely fit that mold in some ways, but I think the perception of my hometown hindered the ability of these students to get to know me. I felt judged by them before they even knew what my values were, and I got the "rich white girl" label. Once I was labeled and perceived in a certain way, I discovered that the other students did not want to be associated with me.

It was during this fall that I first started seeing a psychologist. I was initially sent to the school counselor, whom I had refused to talk when she found out from teachers that I was having conflicts with the other students in my class. When I went to see her, I sat silently on the other side of her office in a chair and I remember staring out the window while telling her that I had nothing to say. So instead, per her recommendation, my parents decided to make me go and see someone in downtown Berkeley once a week. They wanted me to talk to someone and figure out why all of this was going on and why I had been ostracized. My new psychologist, Dr. Mallory, was a tall, blonde, and very pretty lady who was said to be an expert in teenage girls. I ended up seeing her once a week all four years of my high school career. Despite the occasional session where I would "willingly" offer up information about my school life, most of the sessions went something like this: I would go and refuse to speak until she started asking me questions. I would then answer the questions in as few words as possible. Finally, she would give up with the questions and then I would just go on and on about shoes, dresses, vacations, and really any materialistic item I wanted or had. Then she would try and get me to bring up "x" terrible situation that had happened recently at school. Of course, she already knew what happened because my parents had already informed her (they were on a very tight emailing basis), but she wanted me to be the one to tell her about it. In order to appease her, I would acknowledge that yes the incident happened, but that was it. I remember that she would always looked at me with this broken and twisted face and then would say something like, "well aren't you upset about it?" and I would always respond the same way: "it doesn't affect me. I don't feel anything." Then she would say, "everyone has emotions, you must feel something," and I would always reply: "well then I feel indifferent."

I was using denial as a sort of coping mechanism. I kept pretending that I didn't feel anything and that I was happy in my own isolated world, making it incredibly hard for those around me to try and read what I truly felt. I think I genuinely believed that I didn't feel anything and that I was ok. I put all of my energy into obsessing over the materialistic world, because there, everything was perfect. I needed to pretend like nothing was wrong and that I had the perfect life that I was working so hard to portray. I thought the only way for me to fit in was to make it appear to everyone else that I had what I wanted, which was to have the most clothes, the best shoes, and go to the coolest places. I had to get A's and I had to "win" everything. I was obsessed with winning. It didn't matter what it was as long as I could win it. Whether it was getting the highest score on a math test or finishing first at a race, I think "winning" was one of the only times I actually felt good about myself.

I was Anna Feld's top distance runner that year and I had qualified for the state cross-country championship as an individual. I was proud of myself for maintaining the top spot on the team, and even though I didn't have friends at Anna Feld, I think the other runners on the cross country and track team respected me for my athletic ability. I also remember how proud my father was of me for winning MVP as a freshman. My dad had been a Division 1 runner in college, so I wanted to follow in his footsteps and achieve something similar. I thought that by focusing on athletics and becoming a top runner, I would appear to others that I was good enough and worthy of their friendship.

I did such a good job of maintaining that focus that I don't think anyone at school could tell how hurt and alone I was. From the outside, I was materialistically perfect. No one could see through my facade enough to realize that I didn't have the one thing I wanted so desperately: friendship and acceptance from my peers.

In search of this acceptance, I decided to leave the Anna Feld School and transfer into my town's public high school. My hope was that my life would go back to the way it had been in middle school, and that I would be able to eat lunch and spend time with my old group of friends. I was also hopeful that joining the cross-country and track team there would enable me to make even more friends and reach my goal of running at the university level.

3

Until Arcadia

I started practicing with Morgan High's cross-country team two weeks before school started. I was enjoying every minute of it. The team was large, but the varsity girls group was small and competitive. I seemed to fit right in. At the first time trial, I got third, which marked my position as a point scorer for the upcoming season.

The classes at Morgan High were bigger than they had been at Anna Feld, but that was to be expected at any public school of that size. I wouldn't say they were any easier though. As one of the top ten public high schools in California and top 100 in the United States, Morgan

High School academics were no walk in the park. However, I was prepared for them, especially after a year of Anna Feld academics.

I re-connected with my friends from middle school. There were about ten girls in the friend group, but within the ten girls, my closest friends were Kelsey and Emma. On most days at lunch, Kelsey, Emma, and I would eat on a bench separate from everyone else. The three of us got along really well and seemed to pick up where we had left off at the end of 8th grade. The only thing that seemed to strain our friendship was the question of why I left the prestigious private high school that I had been so excited to attend just a year prior. I knew that no one could find out that I had been socially isolated there. If they did, I would die a social death almost instantly. If anyone found out that I left because I couldn't make friends, then they would know that there was something wrong with me. That was the shameful little secret I kept everyday. And so, when I was asked about it, I lied and said I left because I didn't like the academics or the teaching style.

My sophomore year cross-country season was the best season I had in high school. It was full of personal record times, and I was consistently the team's number 3 runner that year. I earned the nickname Luna after one of the other girls decided that I looked like the actress who played Luna Lovegood in the recent *Harry Potter* movie. While I didn't quite see the resemblance, I suppose it was because of my blond wavy hair.

When springtime came, the head coach decided to retire, and someone new was appointed to manage the Track & Field team. He was a distance specialist and had coached collegiate Cross Country and Track prior to coming to Morgan High. He had a long last name, but everyone simply referred to him as "Del".

It came as no surprise to me that track practice ran a little differently than that of cross-country. Everyone was split up into different events: sprinters, distance runners, jumpers, and throwers. Along with the new head coach came two assistant coaches. The one I remember most was Troy, the assistant sprints coach. Troy had also attended Morgan High School and was still pretty young.

Del handled the distance runners, myself included. My main event was the two-mile, but I still occasionally ran the mile. The workouts were hard, and I quickly learned that Del liked to yell. I vividly remember our 3-mile tempo runs on the track. Del would give us our splits and decide who we were running with. Usually we had to finish the workout in under 20 minutes. My times had been dropping, and he wanted me to run with our top milers during workouts. I remember I always started off running with them, but as the workout progressed, I would start to fade and find myself about 20 or 30 meters behind. Whenever this happened, I would be called out on it. In his loud, scary, yelling voice, Del would scream: "Anna what are you doing?! Get it together and catch up right now. Anna right now!" Del's angry voice was a little much for a high school girl like myself, but it was usually enough to make me go into a sprint to catch up to them.

He wasn't always stern and yelling though. Sometimes Del was the complete opposite. I would get to practice and he would greet me and the other distance girls with, "Hi sweetie, how are you today?", in a soft endearing voice. It was a little bit creepy though, as was the amount of time he spent hugging some of my teammates.

However, when any one of us varsity distance runners didn't hit our splits, Del swung the other direction. When Del got mad, he went crazy. I can easily recall a day when one of the distance guys didn't hit his 800-meter splits. Del flew off the handle. He threw his stopwatch across the track, pushed down a couple of hurdles, and then left. Another time he was so upset with the team that he wouldn't talk to any one of us at practice. So we just had to figure out what the workout was supposed to be for the day and do it on our own.

As the track season went on, my times improved, and I got faster. Fast enough to make the cutoff to participate in the most prestigious high school track meet: the Arcadia Invitational. The meet was to take place in Southern California in mid April and high school runners from all over the United States would fly in to participate. I was one of the four fastest milers and so I got to go in the 4 x 1 mile relay.

We got to Arcadia around 11:00 in the morning the day before the track meet. After putting our bags in our room, we decided to eat lunch at a restaurant called Soup Plantation. In addition to the four of us running in the relay, there were a number of sprinters and jumpers who had also qualified for the meet, along with Del's latest up and coming distance runner, whom he had taken as an alternate. All of us walked over together to eat without our coaches. Even though I was with the team, my parents had also traveled down to LA to watch me race. While we were eating lunch, I asked the other girls if their parents were also coming to the meet to watch. Most of them replied that their parents were not coming. My response to that was, "Well, my parents would never miss an opportunity to watch me race." Looking back, this comment did not come across the way I had intended.

Two of the girls on the team left lunch early and the rest of us left to return to the hotel about 15 minutes after them. On the walk back to the hotel, I could see Del walking toward us. He looked angry. When he reached us, he took me by the arm and pulled me aside. In his scary voice he said: "What did you say to your teammate? She's crying and it's all your fault. You have no filter and are out of control." Again, I was taken completely by surprise. I hadn't been aware that I had said or done anything wrong. I replied with a rather puzzled: "What?" not knowing that my look of naïve innocence wasn't going to stop Del from flying off the hammer.

Del made me come back to his room with him to discuss the situation. Then he shut the door and started to yell at me. I remember the sprints coach Troy was also in the room. He didn't say anything to me. He just sat there and watched Del unfold. I was sobbing, and I didn't understand why he was so angry at me. He just kept yelling, and I was hysterically crying. He told me that I was kicked out of the meet and couldn't run in the relay. He also told me that I was a terrible person and that there was something wrong with me. He then proceeded to throw things on the floor in a similar fashion to how he would throw his stopwatch on the ground when we missed our splits during practice. After that, the next thing I remember is my mother taking me to her car still in tears and driving away.

I don't know how long I cried for, but it was at least the whole two-hour drive to my grandparent's house at Palm Springs. My mother was horrified. I was in shock and devastated over not running in the meet like I had expected.

After a few meetings with the school principal about Del's behavior at Arcadia, the school district head was notified, and track wasn't the same. Del kind of apologized and I did return to track practice the following week, but I think the other girls were afraid. Everyone had heard about the blow up at Arcadia, and they didn't know what to say, so they kept their distance from me.

Shortly after track ended and school got out in June, Del was fired. I know that my incident contributed to the decision. However, there were other reasons too. The only other one I knew about was an email sent by the father of a sprinter who had been upset about how Coach Del had treated his daughter at the state meet qualifier, but apparently there had been a whole slew of other things for which he

had also been reported.

4

Just Don't Feel

Sometimes, I wonder if what happened at Arcadia had anything to do with what happened between my friends and I that following summer. I'm sure they found out. Maybe it influenced them to distance themselves from me too. It's something that I will never know for sure. My parents, however, later told me that they think it also had something to do with my meltdown at my 16th birthday party. Looking back on it, I can see that it was a classic Aspergian meltdown. My birthday party had taken place in May, less than a month after the Arcadia Invitational. My mom took four of my friends and I to the Ritz-Carlton in Half Moon Bay to celebrate.

My birthday dinner would take place in the private dining room of the hotel restaurant. I was most excited about my birthday cake. It had been custom designed to match the invitation my friends had received inviting them to the party. Of the four girls I had invited, two of them were of course Kelsey and Emma.

The dinner had been going fine until it was time for cake and presents. The dinner plates were cleared and the waiter came to get the cake, which had been on display in the back of the room. I assumed he went to get it to put my candles in and dim the lights so my friends could sing to me. About 10 minutes later, he came back with slices of cake on plates and began placing them in front of each of my guests. I was mortified. The look on my face went from happy to deeply upset in an instant. Tears filled my eyes as I realized the cake had already been cut without the chance for me to blow out the candles that were supposed to go in. This definitely wasn't a part of the plan I had in mind for a perfect Sweet Sixteen party.

My parents could see what was happening and were quick to usher the plates away and get the rest of the cake back and put candles in it so that I could blow them out. It was too late though. I was already in meltdown mode.

The waiter at the restaurant brought the cake back out and everyone around the table did sing to me, but I was so upset I angrily stared off into the distance as they sang. The rest of the night and while I opened my presents, I was in a terrible mood. My parents kept pulling me aside and telling me to calm down because they could tell my friends didn't like how I was responding and didn't want me to ruin the night or hurt my relationship with them. No one was able to understand why I couldn't just let it go.

Regardless of if it was because of the Arcadia incident, my birthday party, a combination, or some other factors I am unaware of, what I do know is that my two closest friends, Kelsey and Emma, ditched me that summer. They made it clear that I was no longer their friend when they stopped returning my texts and phone calls, and then proceeded to exclude me from both of their summer birthday parties. Instead of me, they hung out with another girl who seemed to have taken my place. One day, when we had planned to go to Jamba Juice together, Emma texted me an hour before we were supposed to meet up and said that she couldn't go anymore because she had already gone with Kelsey. I was upset and confused, but I decided that I would to go and hang out with my cross-country friends once school started.

I started out the year trying to do just that and tried to become closer with a friend from the team that I had run with the previous year. This girl was also a varsity runner and we saw each other at cross-country practice everyday after school. I figured that we had a lot in common with running and that it would be easy to be her friend during the lunch hour. We had even gotten together once during the summer. Upon hanging out at her group's table during the first week at school, I learned that I knew one of her friends from National Charity League, a group of that I was a part of that met on Sundays to do community service. This girl, Penelope, had been in the group with me since sixth grade, so I thought it would be a great opportunity to develop a closer friendship with her. However, a few weeks into the school year, she was the one who started asking me why I wasn't hanging around with Emma and Kelsey anymore. I told her that I had a falling out with them. She seemed adamant that I go and make up with them and even went as far as to contact them herself asking them to make-up with me. She did all of this despite me telling her that it wasn't a real possibility. Looking back, I realize that this was her cue to me that I was unwanted in her lunch group, and it was also her attempt to try and get me to leave without directly saying it to my face.

Despite her attempts to get me to leave her group, I still wanted to be her friend and by the recommendation of my parents and psychologist, I invited her to attend the Jonas Brothers concert with me. It was at the concert that she decided to tell me that I was not welcome to hang out with her friend group at school anymore. She tried to make herself look good by saying, "You are friends with Kelsey and Emma so go and hang out with them. I talked to Kelsey and she wants to eat lunch with you on Monday." It was then clear that I wasn't allowed back, and I felt like she used me for the concert ticket. It was even worse that my mom and I would still have to see Penelope and her mother at National Charity League events and pretend to not have the distaste for them that we did.

The following Monday, I went to lunch and sat down with Kelsey and Emma as planned. It was completely awkward. They didn't talk to me and I didn't talk to them. I sat in silence and offered them some brownies I had made as a friendship reconciliation.

I called my mom on the phone that afternoon before cross-country practice and cried. It was over, and I was done. I didn't know what to do, but I knew that I was now alone.

After that incident, I lived day-to-day with the same routine. I would wake up, get ready for school, and eat breakfast at home. Then I would leave to drive to school with my sister, Sierra, who was a freshman at the time. After arriving to campus and parking my car in the school parking lot, my sister and I would part and go our separate ways. Sierra would go to meet up with her friends before school, and I would keep walking until I reached my locker. From there, I would get the books I needed for the day and head to the library. This is where I would stay until the bell rang for my first class.

I didn't mind being in class. I had some acquaintances with whom I could talk. Then after the first two periods, brunch came. During brunch, most people would find their friends and have a snack, but because I didn't have any friends, I simply went to my next class early.

After another two classes, then the most dreaded part of the day would arrive: lunch. I hated lunch. A billion little cliques that had been together since kindergarten were spread across the large quad eating in circles. Because I had no circle where I was welcome, I avoided that part of campus like the plague. Instead I went to the library. The only challenge with that was that there was no food allowed in the library, so

I usually spent about ten minutes on either end of the lunch period munching away on the benches just outside the entrance. I remember the feeling of shame and fear that was always in the pit of my stomach when I sat out there. I was afraid that people would see me on those benches and know that I had no friends with whom to eat. Sometimes people from my grade would pass by while entering or exiting the library. I knew they saw me there. It felt so wrong and so terrible, yet I didn't know why. Was there something wrong with me that everyone else knew? This wasn't the first time I was socially isolated at school, so I gathered that there was clearly something wrong with me. I simply couldn't wait for lunch to end, so that this awful feeling would go away and I could attend my other classes and work on my homework.

Cross-country season that year sucked. Pretty much every other distance girl had quit the team. Coach T had taken over after Del's removal, and she was kind of a ditz. I didn't understand how she could put up with the attitudes of some of the girls without saying anything to them. I guess she was just very good at looking the other way and pretending like she had no idea what was going on, even when the team captains would opt out of a run and go to the Starbucks instead or hang out in the school parking lot. On top of that, I wasn't running as fast as

I had the year before. I was still on varsity, but my dream of becoming a top distance runner was dwindling away with my increased times. Even my younger sister was beating me.

Finally, when winter came, I had a chance to escape the life that seemed to pain me so much at the time. Since I was a young girl, my family had always traveled to the mountains every weekend to ski. We typically left on Friday afternoons for our mountain home in Squaw Valley and then would return after skiing was over for the day on Sundays. However, when my sister and I got heavily involved in the sport of ski racing, the weekend became a little longer and we would leave on Wednesday or Thursday night after school and return home on Sunday evening after training. The nice part about this was that, from December to April, I was able to get away for almost half of the week. I had a group of friends at Squaw and we did everything together, from skiing to after practice parties. I felt like I was living two completely different lives. At Squaw Valley, I was just a normal teenager with friends that was always included in normal group activities, but when I would go back home on Sunday night, it was a reality check. I hated going back home every week. Additionally, I hated having to lie to my friends at Squaw about my life back home. Like me, the other kids I spent time with at Squaw Valley were only there on the weekends. Everyone was from a different part of the Bay Area where their parents worked and they went to school. Whenever we discussed our lives back home, I made up stories about the "friends" I had there and the things I did with them.

It was especially hard during prom season. The Morgan High prom usually took place in March, when I was still spending my weekends skiing in the mountains. As any normal teenagers would, my Squaw friends and I discussed the proms from various other schools in the Bay Area. Of course they wanted to know who I was going to my prom with. I knew that I wasn't going. I had no one to go with, not even a group of friends. I tried using the excuse that I wasn't dating anybody and didn't have any close guy friends to go with, but then my ski friends, half of them guys, would say, "Why don't you take one of us? We could drive over to your town to go to prom with you." While that was a nice idea, I obviously couldn't do that because then they would know. They would find out the truth about my life at Morgan High School, and consequently would stop being my friend. I couldn't let that happen, so of course I would just say, "Oh well we have a ski race that weekend and I'd rather do that." Being as fast and competitive as I was, no one would argue, because they all knew I loved to win and would never give up a chance to add another medal to my collection.

I'll never forget how hard it was for me to lie to them all of the time, but I definitely could not let them find out the truth, because then I would have no one.

5

I Won't Fall

As the ski season came to an end, track season began. I didn't think my life could get worse, but it did. Since we had a large track team consisting of about 120 runners, the coaches usually selected a handful of us to be captains. I was named as the girls team distance captain (being that I was the only upperclassman among the female distance runners). I was excited to be a captain and it seemed like a great leadership opportunity. In hindsight, I wish I had never been named a captain. The sprint and jump captains hated me, and they made it clear to me that they didn't want me in the mix.

Within the first week of being named the distance captain, I started hearing whispers: *Why is Anna a captain? She shouldn't be a captain.*

I was even approached by the boys' distance captain, Peter. He said: "Anna, you know you shouldn't have been named a captain"... Well then who else would it have been?

Coach T, the same lady who had coached the cross-country team, was the head coach of track and field that year. She was the one who had named me a captain. Since the other captains couldn't change my captain status, they decided to instead exclude me from everything they did as captains -- as if I wasn't already isolated enough.

Everyday, the other six captains would have a meeting without me where they would decide what they were going to have everyone do during practice. Everyday, I would get to practice and have no idea what they were announcing or what was going on. This made me look even worse. Coach T knew what was going on, but she stuck her head in the sand and chose to look the other way.

The first big event that the captains planned was the scavenger hunt. Of course, I wasn't included in the planning of this event, and when I found out about it, it was already too late. The team had been divided into 3 even groups and the fellow distance captain who I was supposed to be working with, Peter, had already planned everything out. He even made another female distance runner on the team an "honorary captain" to help lead the group instead of me. The girl he selected for this role played along and even went to the store and bought matching "leader outfits" to wear on the day of the hunt.

Not too long after the scavenger hunt came the Green and White Meet. Our school colors were green and white and the meet was essentially our time trial. We would divide our team in half (60 and 60) and then compete against each other. Luckily, the two captains who were on my team (the white team) decided to include me in the planning of the T-shirts. They were just using me though; they needed a credit card to order the T-shirts.

I swear that track season was one terrible incident after the next. One day, when I was warming up on the track with a few other distance girls, Troy, who had remained the assistant coach in charge of sprints despite Del's departure, yelled: "Anna why don't you actually act like a captain and go do something useful by moving those hurdles over there." Another time, when the whole team was doing core together in the weight room, he yelled, "Anna, you're doing it all wrong. You're a captain and you can't even hold a plank right." My younger sister, Sierra, who was also on track, had been there to witness his rude comments. She heard them, but didn't say anything back. I remember how sad I had felt when she didn't say anything. I just really needed her to be there for me, but she remained silent in fear of getting called out next.

I remember driving my sister home from practice that day choking back tears. I didn't know what I wanted anymore. I didn't know if I even wanted the situation fixed, how to fix it, or if I even wanted to continue with my sport. In between sobs, I could hear Sierra on the phone with my mother describing the day's events that I didn't want her to know.

There were so many more days just like it. I remember one day when I went to get a foam roller from the shed at the end of the track. I didn't go out there very much, because it was primarily where the jumpers and throwers kept their equipment. Also inside the shed are all of the team photos from every year. When I was in the shed that day, I noticed that there were devil horns drawn on my head from that year's cross-country team photo. I told my parents who then were quick to tell the coach and principal to have the photo removed. The photo may have been taken down, but the image is forever ingrained in my mind.

Growing up, you are told over and over again that actions speak louder than words. So maybe that's why I recall the team picture that year so well. First, the photographer lined everyone up for the giant team picture and when that was finished offered to take smaller group photos. I had gone back to the locker room to use the restroom and when I returned I found every captain, except myself, lined up and posing for the camera. I wasn't quite sure how to handle the situation so I decided to approach the photographer. I tapped her on the shoulder said, "Excuse me, what are you doing?" The photographer replied: "I'm taking a photo of the team captains." I sucked it up, held my breath and replied, "Well I'm a captain so shouldn't I be in it too?" I remember watching her facial expression change. She looked at the other captains completely puzzled as to why they hadn't said anything or gone looking for me before she had started taking photos. She then had me join in with the rest of them and snapped a couple more.

That evening, my mom emailed the photographer and every "captains" photo that didn't have me in it was deleted so that no one could purchase a "captains minus Anna" picture. While that didn't fix the event itself, at least they couldn't get the picture they wanted.

The team photo was definitely the last straw for me. I did not want to continue. I wanted to quit right then and there, but my parents made me finish out the season. They said that because I was a team captain, I was a team leader; therefore it would look bad if I left before track was over. They said that, in my role, it was important that I demonstrate good sportsmanship. While I understand that this is true, the same could not be said about the other captains. They certainly weren't showing good sportsmanship. How could they call themselves team leaders?

After the season ended, my family left the country to travel to Switzerland. Not too far into the trip, I went for a walk with my dad. We sat down together at a café along the street and started talking about running. Apparently Coach T had emailed my dad to let him know that I couldn't be a cross-country captain for my upcoming senior year after what had happened that spring. Even though I was certain that I wanted to quit running anyway, I still felt a new hole begin to develop in my already empty heart. That was what I always wanted to be. I really wanted to be a cross-country captain, so I told my dad that I was done. I was done running. What was the point? I wasn't even fast anymore, so I might as well quit.

6

Out of Reasons to Wake Up

Life went on and by senior year I had no hope for the future. Back

then, I would have said that I wasn't sad and that I didn't feel anything

at all. However, deep down I think I knew that something was wrong.

Senior year felt similar to junior year except for the fact that I had quit

running just like I said I would. Well, I quit racing at least. There was no

going back after the previous track season. I couldn't bear to show my

face. So instead, everyday after school, I drove my little light blue

convertible bug into the Berkeley hills to a trail called Inspiration Point.

I loved Inspiration Point. I would park my car in the small parking lot

that overlooked both the Briones and San Pablo Dam Reservoirs. From there I would take off running down the trail. I was usually alone on the path in the early afternoons, but it was one of the only times in the day where I felt like I belonged. It was such a nice place to run. From the left side of the trail I could see a beautiful view of the Golden Gate Bridge and to the right of the trail the Briones Reservoir. A couple of miles in, I would reach the point where cows roamed around freely and cattle gates crossed the path every quarter mile. Finally, a mile beyond that, was when I knew I was far enough away that no one else was around. That's where I would stop running, feel my eyes start to water, and start to cry. Then I would turn around, run back, and drive home like it was just another normal day.

Of course, I was still meeting with my psychologist once a week. I still never talked about school, but since I had been seeing Dr. Mallory every week for a few years now, I thought I might as well talk about something. So I used the time to talk about all of the things about my family that irritated me. I mean there's always some sort of family drama going on. The time passed a little quicker this way and years later she told me that she was surprised at how easy it was for me to talk about my family, but then when it came to school and my real feelings, I was like a brick wall. You could talk to me, but you would get nothing back. It's like there was nothing there, which she told me later on made it really hard for her to read me. And if I was incredibly hard to read for one of the top child adolescent psychologists in the greater Bay Area, then I sure must have put on a good show for those around me.

I could tell that she wanted me to let her in. She wanted to understand what was going on inside my head, but I wouldn't let her. I wouldn't let anyone. My parents weren't allowed in my therapy sessions, but they sent Dr. Mallory many emails that I would logon to my mom's computer to read when she wasn't home. I wanted to know what my parents were saying about me. I had a feeling that there was something wrong with me that no one was telling me, and I wanted to know what it was. The emails were about all sorts of things that came up, but usually read something like: "Dr. Mallory, We are concerned about Anna and she doesn't seem to want to talk to us. Can you please talk to her about this next week?" Dr. Mallory's response was always something along the lines of: "Anna seems to be doing ok at the moment. The way she is choosing to deal with what she is facing at school seems to be keeping her happy and I don't think we should push her to talk. We need to wait. When she's ready, she'll decide to talk about it." When I read these emails I was always satisfied because this meant that I was winning at my own little mind game I was playing. Dr. Mallory was on my side, and as long as she didn't make me talk, I could just keep living in my perfect emotionless world.

However, even though Dr. Mallory never made me talk about the things I couldn't, I think she was worried about my psychological wellbeing and wanted to help me. I missed one of my classes every week at school to attend my appointment with her in the middle of the day. I always thought it was a nice break from academics and I felt lucky to be able to go somewhere while the rest of my classmates were busy studying. Sometimes at the end of our appointment, she would take me to this fancy ice cream shop called Ici. It was on the famous College Avenue in Berkeley and only one block from her office. It always had a long line out the door and their cones were handmade and dipped in chocolate. I loved that.

On my way home from my appointment, particularly if it had been a day where I had to talk about one of the incidents at school, I would turn on the stereo in my little car to play my favorite song, "Mean," by Taylor Swift. It's funny how singing out loud to your life's current theme song has this way of releasing some of that pressure and tension that you feel.

And then there was group. Dr. Mallory had really wanted me to join this so called "group" that she led on Tuesday nights. Group. Was. Interesting. I was the only girl among three boys. First there was Tommy. He appeared to be somewhat normal and often talked about his small group of friends that he liked to hang out with at his charter high school. Then there was Jason. He played the guitar and the piano. I remember that. He was so quiet and definitely the painfully shy type. I knew he was smart though, because he went to one of the prestigious Bay Area private high schools. And finally there was Calvin. He was definitely the storyteller. He was from Berkeley and I think he was home-schooled. I know he had been caught up with the police multiple times based on what he said about being on some sort of probation. Between the four of us it was definitely an odd mix. Especially since I was always trying to be "little miss perfect," because I thought I was "too good" for group. Group always started with one of us picking a conversation topic and then going off of that. We had some pretty interesting conversations during group. The ones I remember the most were stories told by that boy Calvin. After being in a group with him, I came to the conclusion that if I had problems, they were minor in comparison to his. I remember one night when he told us about how his girlfriend would throw up in jars and then put them underneath her bed. I'm pretty sure he was serious about it too. The fun part about group was that when it was someone's birthday or right before a holiday, Dr. Mallory would take us outside and walk with us to the Beanery Café to celebrate with pastries and treats. We must've looked like the funniest group of teenagers walking down College Avenue with this pretty blonde lady who probably could have passed for someone's mother. Even though the group was a little weird, I kind of liked it.

As the days of my senior year wore on, it felt like my existence was becoming increasingly pathetic. I began to feel lost in a giant dark world. Getting up and going to school everyday was becoming harder and harder. I needed a reason to keep going and waking up every day because I thought that was it. I thought my life was never going to change. Even amidst the college application process and being admitted to my top choice university in the Midwest, I was unsure of whether or not the glimmer of hope I saw for the future was real.

Even though I didn't talk about how much pain I was in emotionally, I think my mom could see that I was sad. I had begged and begged to transfer schools again after my junior track season had turned out so horribly. I couldn't though. My parents wouldn't let me. They told me that transferring schools again would look bad on my college application and decrease my chances of getting into a top school. So to make up for the fact that I had to stick it out at Morgan High, she would pull me out of school for the day and take me places. She would say things like, "Anna I called you in sick today to school. We're going to Napa instead." And there we would spend the day driving up and down Silverado Trail and shopping in St. Helena.

That was around the time that I found Demi. Demi Lovato had recently come out of rehab and I kept hearing about it on the news. I was intrigued by her story and wondered what had caused her to go to rehab in the first place. After a little bit of research, I discovered that Demi had problems growing up that had caused her to have an eating disorder and self-harm issues, all of which ultimately landed her in the treatment center that she was now publicly talking about on television. Out of all of the things she said in her interviews, what really stuck out to me was when she described how she felt like she was "living a lie" and had to smile everyday and pretend like everything was ok and just keep going when it wasn't. That was exactly how I felt. In almost every interview I watched of Demi she said, "It gets easier. You just have to keep going." So I kept going. I didn't let myself fall any deeper than I already was during my senior year. I wanted so badly to quit school, but I kept going because Demi said it would get better.

I held on to those words, and after what seemed like an eternity of miserable Morgan High School days, I did finally make it to the end of the tunnel. I graduated from high school, and as I walked across the football field with my diploma, I told myself I was never going to set foot on that campus again.

7

Closer to the Stars

I absolutely loved going on trips when I was in high school. I wanted to

get as far away as possible to escape the reality I faced in my

hometown. I liked to travel to exotic places where I could "forget" the

events of the previous school year and distract myself from my feelings

of guilt and shame of not being good enough.

The summer I graduated from high school, my family took a

trip to Africa to climb Mt. Kilimanjaro and go on a safari. My sister and

I were not super excited to climb Kilimanjaro because, frankly, a

weeklong camping trip up a tall mountain in the middle of Africa just

didn't sound that appealing to us. We would have much rather skipped

the mountain climbing part and just gone on the safari. However, the deal my parents made with us was that, in order to go on the safari, we also had to climb Kilimanjaro as a family as a 50th birthday present to my mother. So grudgingly, Sierra and I agreed to the climb. It's not like we really had that much of a choice.

Being a long distance runner, I didn't think much about the climb until I arrived in Tanzania to begin. I figured that if I could run long distances, I could surely climb a 20,000 foot mountain. In hindsight, I admit that I ought to have done some of my own research prior to embarking on the trip because climbing "Kili", as the locals call it, was no walk in the park. It turned out to be a testing seven days and six nights of trekking and camping at high elevations where I encountered constant dirt, no showers, and altitude sickness. The first two days of the climb went ok for me, but I watched my sister get really sick within that first 24 hours. Little did I know that I was next. It was the 14,000 foot mark on the third day that got me. By the fourth day, I laid sick and miserable in my tent, planning my escape down the mountain to my fantasy five star hotel that probably didn't even exist in the small town of Arusha. Finally, the next morning, I woke up feeling a little better and I realized it would be stupid to forgo summiting the mountain a mere day and a half from the top. So, as delusional as I was from refusing to eat any of the food our cook made for fear of getting sick again, I put on a determined face and decided to suck it up and reach the top.

It takes around seven hours to reach the summit from the last base camp, so most people beginning the trek in the early hours of the morning. The morning my family summited the mountain, it was freezing cold. I was wearing two or three ski parkas on top of my layers of long johns. My toes were completely frozen despite the many hand warmers I kept adding into my boots. I couldn't feel my feet at all, but that didn't seem to matter to anyone in my family or to any of our guides. They were all in a "shut up and climb" mood. To combat my frustration with them, I ended up trekking off ahead of everyone to be by myself. Of course one of our three guides took off after me to follow close behind. As I got nearer to the crater rim, each step became more difficult from the increase in altitude and the decrease in available oxygen. Every couple of steps, I would stop for a brief moment to catch my breath and look up into the sky. I had never seen so many stars in my life. I was so high up that I could clearly and vividly see the whole Milky-Way band stretched across the sky. Seeing the dark night sky like that changed me. It made me realize that I'm just one speck in a massive universe and all of the problems in the universe make my own seem less significant in comparison to so many others.

When I finally hit the outer rim of the crater at Stella Point, it was a complete blizzard. I was still a good 40 minutes from Uruhu Peak. I remember having this "oh shit" moment when I realized that I still had 40 minutes left to get to the sign that marked the top. I was the most uncomfortable I had ever been. I couldn't feel my feet, it was a complete blizzard, and I sure didn't want to keep going. I wanted to sit down and cry, but I trekked on anyway. I mean my guide had already done this hike twenty times and he was still alive. So I kept going and arrived at the sign, a grand total of 19,341 feet, at 5:45 am.

After getting my picture in front of the sign, I ran down the mountain with my Kenyan guide, the one who had gone with me when I had split away from my family much earlier in the morning.

Climbing Mt. Kilimanjaro was one of the hardest weeks of my life both mentally and physically. It taught me that I can endure physical pain, camping, and the feeling that I will not make it out alive.

I definitely forgot about the pain of my hometown for the time being, but I also learned that life was so much bigger than the issues back home. Through the climb, I had the chance to meet many wonderful Tanzanians that had been a part of our crew. We had a team of twenty people including cooks, guides, tent-carriers, guys who carried my luggage up the mountain on their heads, and much more. However, most of them only got paid $100 USD for the whole week. To put that in perspective, every member of my family's crew went through the same climb my family did, had to carry all of our stuff, and then got paid next to nothing for it. It was their job. I learned that they endure this climb a couple of times each month. They get just as sick as we do during the climb, and they can't even afford the mounds of medication and painkillers that my parents had brought with us to help make the trek just a little bit easier.

I still vividly remember one night during the climb when my mom was talking to our cook. He had complained to her of altitude sickness and a headache. After talking with him for awhile, my mom realized that he probably wasn't taking anything for it and offered him two Advil pills from the large bottle we had brought with us. I'll never forget the look of relief I saw in his eyes when he gratefully accepted them from her.

It was even more shocking for me to find out that these guys weren't even considered poor. Being a part of a Kilimanjaro crew was considered good pay. For the first time, I was able to see a problem that was worse than any problem I had faced in school. It made me realize that I should be grateful for my life, because, even though I thought there was nothing to live for, at least I had a nice home, a family who loved me, and I didn't have to worry about how I was going to physically survive.

Part 2

A New Beginning

8

In a Moment

"I've heard it said, that people come into our lives for a reason."[1] If it wasn't for every person I crossed paths with while attending university, I wouldn't be where I am today. It's the place where I saw myself grow and change as a person in a direction I never believed I would.

When I arrived at university, I was afraid. I was afraid of being rejected again, I was afraid of being isolated, and I was afraid of being alone. I didn't think college was going to be any different than high

---

[1]Schwartz, Stephen. "For Good." Wicked: Original Broadway Cast Recording, Decca Broadway, 2003.

Wicked is one of my favorite musicals because it tells a story about a girl who was different. I have always been different, so I found it only fitting to start this chapter with a quote from Wicked that sums up my experience at university.

school had been. My memories and experiences of child and adolescent schooling were riddled with incidents of being misunderstood by teachers, rejected by peers, and left out. Why then, would I believe that another place would be any different?

However, it was here that I first saw a glimpse of hope for myself. I was surprised at how nice people were. Many girls started reaching out to me and inviting me to the dining hall, because they wanted to be my friend. I thought, *but wait? Isn't there something wrong with me? Can't these people also see that I am below them?* I didn't understand why they were being so nice to me. I was so used to being ignored and isolated that I wasn't sure what to think of it. Right before my very eyes, my life was drastically changing.

Within a matter of weeks, I made an amazing group of friends that lived in my dorm. And it wasn't just a few girls. There were eleven of us total. I had not just one, but many girls to talk to. I was going to lunch and dinner with them everyday and it felt so good to be included. I felt like I had waited for centuries to just sit at a table with friends at lunch and now it was happening as if it were just a normal thing.

Since I was attending a Catholic institution, one of the unique things about studying there was that there was a chapel in every single dorm. Usually the dorm had mass two times per week: once on a weekday and once on Sundays. Mass in my particular dorm was on Sunday evenings at 10pm since that was what worked best with people's study schedules. Even though I wasn't Catholic, I started to attend mass on a weekly basis, because my friend's were going and I wanted to connect with them and see what it was all about.

At the same time that all of this was happening, I decided to try-out to walk onto the rowing team. I hadn't been planning on it, but had been handed a brochure one evening with try-out meeting times. I was looking for ways to get involved and meet more people so I thought, "Why not?" The tryout process was long, but after about 2 months of sticking it out, I received an email congratulating me that I made the team as a coxswain. Now, I didn't just have one group of friends, but two. I think joining the rowing team made me feel like I belonged somewhere. All of the freshmen rowers and coxswains ate dinner together after practice in the dining hall. On many days, simply going to practice made me feel loved and wanted. Everyone was so nice to me. Almost like a family. The way a team should be. I was also excited that one of the other girls who had made the team as a coxswain lived in my dorm. Sometimes, I would see her in the laundry room and we would chat about rowing. It was really nice to be able to have something in common to talk about with her. She had also been a runner in high school, so, in addition to rowing, we shared very similar backgrounds.

However, at the same time that I started to feel more connected to myself again, I realized that I was also suffocating and longing to be free. I was living as a materialistic version of myself that I had worked so hard to craft and maintain over the previous four years. Maybe I didn't need to hide behind her anymore. I had pretended for so long to be this perfect person that I wasn't. In reality, I was incredibly weak from having been torn down so many times. I had been putting so much pressure on myself to be perfect and to give the impression to others like I had everything I wanted... yet underneath this beautiful image that I had created, I was only a shattered window, where the frame was left standing.

9

Lies

For a long time, I thought I was bulletproof. The truth is that as much as I'd like to think that nothing ever affected me, it did. No one is bulletproof. It's just a matter of time before you eventually break. I couldn't keep pretending that things didn't affect me, because they did. I had become so talented at blending in and covering up for the fact that high school had been a nightmare for me.

My high school experience was affecting me, even if it wasn't in the ways I had initially thought it would. There were so many emotions surfacing at once that I didn't know what they all were or what to do with them. I was confused, sad, and angry. So I decided to journal. I just wrote down exactly how I felt about every moment along with everything that crossed my mind. I knew that I needed to talk about it so I ended up reading them to Dr. Mallory who I still talked to every week on the phone. I remember the time when I first brought up my emotions with her. She definitely wasn't expecting it. It must have been confusing for her that after years of silence, one day I just decided to open up about something that I refused to discuss or even acknowledge the existence of before. I suppose I decided to open up, not because I was ready, but because I just couldn't hold it in.

I left these notes on my desk in my room, which probably wasn't the best place to keep them since I had a roommate.

The Friday night before our first finals week, my roommate, Kendall, came up to our room sobbing. She asked me to go down to talk to the Sister with her. Once we were in the rectress' apartment, Kendall proceeded to have a hysterical breakdown. Through all of her tears she choked out that she was extremely worried about me. She read the pile of notes that I had left on my desk. It was clear that my writing had scared her. Just as I had managed to tell her that everything was fine and not to worry, the phone in the apartment rang. The rectress answered it and proceeded to tell whoever was on the other end that everything was fine and not to worry. It sounded serious, and I was curious as to who was on the other end. When she hung up the phone, the rectress told us that it was the police. They had received a call from my roommate's parents, who were worried about her mental stability after she had called them in tears. It was then that I realized I wasn't the only one having a hard time. Of course, the rectress then had my roommate call her parents and tell them that she was ok before we continued discussing the notes.

I left the meeting thinking we had worked everything out, but then 5 days later my roommate informed me that she was switching rooms. When I asked her why, she said that it was because our schedules didn't match up. She said that she wanted to stay friends despite living in different rooms the next semester and even offered to set up a weekly lunch date. I knew that wasn't the real reason she had decided to leave though. It just didn't seem to make sense. When I got back from winter break, I asked her again, but she still said the same thing. She was lying to my face. Finally, when she did tell me the truth about why she switched rooms, she said it was because my writing sounded suicidal and was scared not knowing what I was going to do next. Also, she said she couldn't deal with "me and my crap" and that two emotionally unstable people can't live in the same room. From that comment, I gathered that she considered us both emotionally unstable. Either way, that was the end of that and was one of the last times I ever spoke to her.

I retreated back to my teammates and my group of friends in the dorm after that incident. I told all of my new friends what had happened from my point of view because I knew that on the other end, my old roommate, was busy telling all of her friends that I was emotionally unstable. I was worried that if they heard her side of the story first, they would stop being my friend. However, much to my benefit, every person I told was very understanding of the situation and reassured me that my next roommate would probably be nicer anyway. Yet somehow, I still felt scared. Now that I knew what it felt like to be loved and accepted by others, I never wanted to go back to how things had been before. The fear that lived in the back of my mind was that at any moment all of my new friends would discover that I was unworthy of friendship and would turn on me. The fears then manifested themselves into nightmares as I embarked on my own emotional roller coaster – an endless roller coaster that seemed to only be beginning.

On the one hand, things were going so well. I was socializing with my peers, making friends, and a valued member on a team. I was eating meals at the dining hall with friends, going to social events, and attending Catholic masses. A few of my friends were very committed Catholics, and so going to mass with them became a part of my weekly routine. Sometimes I would go with them even more than once a week. There was mass somewhere every day of the week, and each mass had it's own theme. There was Chili mass, Waffle Wednesday mass, and my personal favorite, Milkshake Mass Thursday.

However, in addition to indulging in all of these fun events, I was suffering from anxiety and fear of what was going to happen next. *Would I keep my new friends? Would university continue to be a place where I was loved and accepted?* These are just a few of the questions that turned over and over in my mind. Returning home during breaks was a challenge. After all, I was going back to the place where I had been isolated, alone, and without friends after finally having found somewhere where people accepted me.

I can vividly recall a day during winter break of freshman year when I had gone with my mom to pick up my sister from school. As we pulled into the parking lot, I was on the verge of tears. I couldn't help but stare at the benches in front of the library where I had eaten alone everyday for two years. It was remarkable how quickly that knot was able to return. The knot was in the pit of my stomach and was the same one that I used to have everyday as I walked through the hallways feeling inadequate and alone. Only the difference was that this time, it felt worse because I knew that high school didn't have to be the way that I had previously experienced it. I knew that there were actually nice people in the world who genuinely wanted to be my friend.

Whenever the feeling returned, it always seemed to come out of nowhere, even though I knew that wasn't really the case. There were definitely certain places, situations, and comments that triggered it. Usually any place, person, or situation that even remotely reminded me of my high school.

It should come as no surprise that the feeling returned the day I went with some new friends from the rowing team to volunteer at a local elementary school. Our job for the day was to paint murals in the auditorium that would later be hung outside of the school facing the street. Even though I was in the auditorium in a different setting, just standing inside of it reminded me of standing in the Morgan High School auditorium. Every time I had to go into that auditorium, it was for an assembly or a school rally. Back in my high school days, I hated assemblies and rallies. I hated anything that involved the whole school sitting in the auditorium because it gave me a feeling of inadequacy. You see, even though I had my acquaintances from class, as soon as we entered the auditorium, all that mattered was your friends from kindergarten. Everyone would leave their classmates with whom they had walked over, and find their Kindergarten friend group. I had no friends from Kindergarten. I had moved to that suburb in the 5th grade, and even then, I stayed at the same private school I had been attending until I reached the 7th grade. So for me, going to assemblies and rallies was like putting salt in all of the cuts that were already there. Rubbing in every awful aspect of my pathetic social situation and high school isolation.

However, despite the many experiences that proved difficult for me to face, there were also new, good experiences that fulfilled a need that had been sitting empty inside of me for so long. When the dorm formal came, it felt like the high school prom I never went to. I had a date and many friends to go with. My friends and I took pictures together before the dance in our beautiful dresses to post on Facebook, went to dinner together, and finally made our way to a club at the top of the stadium where the dance would take place. It was almost surreal to be able to actually go to a formal with friends after never going in high school.

Amidst the positive energy surrounding my happiness to have been included in the event, I called my mom on the phone the next day in tears. I was just so confused. A big part of me still didn't understand why it had to be so awful before, but different now. *Now I could just go to formals like a normal person and have a fun time?* I was still the same person. So why didn't I get to be included in this fun before?

That winter I also joined the university's club ski team. Through the ski trips, I grew close to one of the older girls on the team, Hadley. I really looked up to Hadley and I told her about my struggles in high school and my insecurities about my new friends. She seemed to have taken an interest in me and seemed to have decided that I was going to be "her freshman." Later on in the year, she referred to me as her "project child". I was deemed the "project child" because it was generally expected that everyone who joins the ski team likes to drink alcohol. The problem was that I didn't drink alcohol. At least, not yet anyway. Despite this, I was still accepted onto the team because of the incredible times I had posted at tryouts. I was, by far, the fastest one

My friends knew something was wrong because I had stopped going to meals with them. They barely saw me because I always had excuses to avoid them and any questioning comments they may have had. It didn't matter to me much anyway, since I felt like my plan was working. I was getting boated more and more and getting to practice with the team instead of riding in the launch.

However, the problem with not eating is that, when you're not eating enough, the chemicals in your brain are imbalanced and you can't think as clearly. You start to lose control of what you're doing. My anxiety was increasing from the lack of food and the fact that I still hadn't mastered the art of the social nuances of the girls on my team. I had been talking to one of my coxswain friends who I liked about rooming together in an apartment senior year, since most students make these arrangements during their sophomore year. My friends from my dorm were all planning on living in the dorm as seniors and I wanted to live off campus, which is why I had gone to my rowing friends to see if any of them wanted to live off with me. The girl I asked had seemed interested at first, but then later on told me that she was planning to room with the other coxswain from my team and that they were only getting a two-bedroom apartment. I was sad, but I supposed that the other girl who hadn't been very warm to me just didn't want me in their mix. This suspicion was later confirmed when another teammate of mine, a rower, mentioned two months later that she would be living with these two girls senior year in a three-bedroom apartment. Hurt, I asked the twin sister of one of the coxswains who was in the apartment about what had happened and she replied: "yes I'm sorry we lied, we just didn't want to hurt your feelings." *Whatever.* Like that hadn't happened to me fifty times before in my life already.

To get back at the other coxswains in my class for being so exclusive and cliquey towards me, I wanted to beat them. Yes, two of them were being boated ahead of me for the time being, but the one girl was only being boated ahead because she was lighter... Not because she was a better coxswain. That's what some of the other girls were telling me at least. So I continued down my path of starvation. I was determined to make myself lighter or at least equally as light as the coxswain who was coxing one of the boats ranked ahead of mine so that I would have a greater chance of beating her.

As my diet continued to decrease in size, my temper shortened and my decision-making process began to decrease in quality. I was so anxious that I decided I would rather be unconscious so that I wouldn't have to deal with the anxieties and constant chatter in my head anymore. I had a plan. I was going to overdose and I knew exactly how much of what to take because I had researched it. It had started out as just a thought, but then it got darker and deeper until one night the impulse to do it was so strong that I ended up hiding all of the pills from myself to make it harder to follow through.

Around the same time I was experiencing these thoughts, I had a running accident. I went on an 11 mile run before my afternoon rowing practice and I fell on some loose gravel six miles into the run. I broke three of my permanent teeth, which took a year and three dental surgeries later to fix. There was blood everywhere. It covered my arms and legs and kept coming out of my mouth. The first dental surgery was the same day. Luckily they were able to do a root canal and put fake teeth on so that I didn't have to walk around smiling with a gap in my mouth.

Most of the people I knew at the time thought that I had lied about the accident. They believed that I had passed out when I was running so I was invited to somewhat of an eating disorder intervention meeting with my rowing coaches the following week. They had called the team doctor and had arranged an appointment at the health center for me for an eating disorder evaluation. The appointment was the day before I left for Thanksgiving break. I was so frightened that my close friend and teammate, Emmie, walked me there. I remember when we got there I turned to Emmie and said, "Maybe I'll just not go." Emmie's response was "When was the last time you ate?" I replied, "yesterday" and then she said, "yeah um you should probably go." I eventually went in, but I denied all forms of an eating disorder and all the behaviors I had been using. Yet I still somehow managed to walk out of there with an order for my first set of labs. Later on, I would learn these would be the first of many.

The following day, I flew to Vail, Colorado for Thanksgiving with my family. I got off the plane and fell into my dad's arms. The first thing he said when he saw me was: "Don't lose anymore weight. You don't look healthy anymore." I didn't know what to say, but I knew that if I didn't tell my parents what was happening, I might not make it. My mom was waiting for my dad and I on the living room couch when we arrived at the condo late that night. I was tired and scared, so I curled up next to her and stayed there until morning. My parents knew something was terribly wrong and over the next couple of days I somehow managed to tell them that the rowing coaches had forced me to get blood tests at the doctor because they thought I was sick. My family usually eats dinner in a restaurant on Thanksgiving and this year was no different. I ate the food, but my mom followed me to the bathroom right after dinner to make sure I didn't throw it up. I didn't throw it up, but I think she was really worried.

A week after I returned from break was the first time I overdosed on laxatives. I took 10 pills at once because I was so freaked out that I had eaten 3 cookies. I passed out, got very sick, and scared the crap out of myself. After finding out about it the next day, a close friend from my dorm came to my room and confiscated the rest of my boxes of pills. So that was that. But then I did it again and a number of additional times over the next couple of months.

When I came home for Christmas break, my eating disorder was definitely a problem, but I didn't think it was. On the second day back home, my parents took me to see an eating disorder dietitian that had been recommended by my psychologist Dr. Mallory, who I still was doing weekly phone sessions with when I was away at school. Dr. Mallory knew I was having eating problems, but she wasn't a specialist in that area and wanted me to see one. That was an appointment I'll never forget. I was completely uncooperative like usual and told the dietitian that I was going to do whatever I wanted, which at the time was losing weight. Based off of my stubborn attitude and what others had told her, the dietitian told my parents right in front of me that I was going to die if they let me go back to school. She said that sending me back to school at my stage was a bad idea because they would be paying for me to go and starve myself since there wouldn't be anyone there to monitor my food intake. She put me on exercise restriction and even went as far as to pull me from my ski trip. I had planned to go skiing in Canada with Emmie during the break and now I could only go as long as I was sedentary. So the next three and a half weeks of Christmas break turned into my parents forcing me to eat everything we ate. They wouldn't let me leave the dinner table without eating enough of every food group. Since I wasn't allowed to run, I went on super long fast-paced walks to try and burn calories. My parents would then drive around the neighborhood looking for me to make sure that I wasn't running. And I certainly can't forget that I had to go to the doctor every week to be "medically monitored" for the first time in my life. So I complied with what my parents wanted and ended up gaining 4 pounds so that they allowed me to go back to school. Well at least they thought

I complied. I was an exceptional liar and was able to get away with stuff that, if others had known, I probably wouldn't have been allowed back.

My mom flew to the Midwest with me to set me up with a doctor at school. At that first meeting with my mom and I, the doctor said something that I have never forgotten. She said: "I have so many girls who struggle with this and they come back years later when they are better and tell me that they wish they hadn't wasted their college years being so consumed in their eating disorder." I knew at the time that I didn't want this to be me, but I was so sick at the time I didn't want to be better either.

So yes by, mid-January I had gained a measly 4 pounds and was eating more, but I was still consumed with thoughts of food and losing weight. My obsession with a certain number was still so important to me. For two months, I kept a wall covered in sticky notes with self-hate messages and whether or not to eat written on them. It was probably one of the weirdest things I ever did, but in my defense I was starving and "a starving brain can't make good decisions" as one of my psychologists back then used to say.

One Saturday in February, I was so consumed with my eating disorder that I decided to lay on the floor of my room all day and not eat because I thought my existence was pathetic. I succeeded at not eating until 6pm when one of my close friends from my dorm dragged me out to eat dinner with her.

I can vividly recall a freezing cold February night when I was barely eating. I wanted to get away with it so badly that when my parents started to express their concern to me about my eating habits, I ran down to the campus health center in the middle of a huge blizzard. It was already 6pm and the center was closing up for the evening. I went to the administrator and revoked all of my consent forms that I signed so that my mom could speak with my doctor there because she had threatened to call her and ask for an update on my health. I knew that I wasn't doing any better and I was afraid of getting caught and pulled out of school.

On another one of those stormy nights, I walked myself through the snow to the campus student center where there were multiple eateries including a Starbucks. I went to the little general store and bought a giant Halloween candy sized bag of chocolates. I remember feeling anxious. I was anxious from not eating that whole day, anxious about school, anxious about getting caught, and anxious about continuing with my eating disorder. I kept eating them all night until two teammates took it away from me already half empty. They told me I had completely lost it and that eating that much chocolate would make me sick.

My weight wasn't stable at all. It kept fluctuating over the next couple of months from all of the cycling between restricting, eating, and purging that I was doing. The time I realized that I actually needed to get better was a few days before I went to Tennessee for spring break. I went to the doctor for my usual appointment. After all, you have to go to the doctor every couple of weeks when you have an eating disorder. One of the things they do at your appointment is check your orthostatic vital signs. First they take your blood pressure lying down and then you stand up for two minutes and they do it again. Only this time my numbers were orthostatic. According to the criteria published in the American Academy of Pediatrics, if I could have been admitted to the hospital for cardiac monitoring. However, where I was studying in the Midwest, they didn't use this standard eating disorder protocol, so I was just sent to the lab to get blood tests to see if I was "medically stable" enough electrolyte-wise to go on the spring training trip to Tennessee. The lab tests came back ok and I was allowed to go, but I think that scared me. It scared me enough to make me realize that I wasn't healthy and I needed to try harder.

I did try a little harder after that. I deleted my calorie counter off of my phone after religiously recording every calorie I ate down to a teaspoon of cinnamon on my apples for almost 8 months. Of course, I could still count calories in my head, but it was a little more difficult to keep track of. I also stopped weighing myself every day, and I tried to eat every meal.

A few weeks after I had stopped stepping on the scale all of the time, I looked in the mirror and saw something different. I saw a girl who was skinny enough, and who didn't need to lose any weight. I had never seen that girl before, but then I saw her again in a picture with her friends, and I remember thinking, *Maybe I am small enough.*

11

Finding a Bigger Purpose

The same year I started battling my eating disorder was the year I decided to convert to Catholicism. After spending most of my life as an Episcopalian, I went through the RCIA process; short for The Rite of Catholic Initiation for Adults. During that year, I was frequently asked why I made the decision to convert. When people asked me this question, I always gave a simple answer and responded with: "I really liked mass my freshman year" or "I finally seemed more connected with God." In reality, it was so much deeper than that for me. The real reason has a lot to do with the changes I went through upon coming to university. When I first came to university, it was the first time I was accepted by my peers. I had been accepted by other girls my own age, many of whom genuinely wanted to be my friend. Their actions were so genuine and their values were so different than what I had grown up with in my wealthy Bay Area suburb. Many of these girls whom I had only just met talked about their faith in a way that I desperately wanted to know and understand. At the same time I was also trying to find closure with the drama that occurred in high school and going to mass gave me this kind of peace within myself that enabled me to come to terms with there being no real explanation for the terrible chain of events I had experienced. It allowed me to accept that maybe bad things happen and there is no reason for it. Going to mass also taught me that maybe I wasn't alone the whole time and God had been supporting me throughout my life even when I didn't know it.

I think it only takes one person to help another person. So I decided to join the Catholic faith so that one day I could be that person who helps someone else and shows them that they don't have to be alone anymore.

Going through RCIA brought me closer with one of my dorm friends who became my sponsor and connected me with the church community that accepted me for who I was.

12

Relapse

By the spring of my sophomore year of college, I was doing much better. My weight had stabilized and I was eating much more frequently and much more than I had been eating all year. However, right as I was turning that critical corner in my recovery, the semester ended and I flew to London to study abroad for the first part of the summer.

Looking back, I don't think going to live in London after being sick and in treatment for an eating disorder was the best idea. Prior to leaving for London, I had been seeing a physician, psychologist, and dietitian weekly. Together they made up my treatment team. When I got to London, I was no longer seeing my treatment team. My physician had written down a few names of doctors for me to see in the UK before I left, but I of course discarded all of their names and numbers immediately upon receiving them since I didn't want to go. And although I thought about it, I of course didn't pack my scale for fear of my flat mates finding out that I had an eating disorder.

After being in London for less than a week, I found that not knowing my weight actually ended up increasing my anxiety. I thought I was growing fatter by the day. I knew I had to eat in front of these girls so they wouldn't know I had a problem, but at the same time I needed a way to get rid of the calories. The flats were small and I knew the other girls would hear me throwing up if I chose to purge that way, so of course I didn't. I chose laxatives. I bought boxes of them from the drugstore, Boots, and took multiple of them everyday. I was getting out of control again and I knew it. I also ran 8-10 miles every day and was sure that my flat mates thought I was one of those crazy runner types. Which was partly true, but probably not to the extent that I was running. If I did not get in at least 8 miles a day I would have a panic attack and make up for it the next day by spending extra time at the gym.

After I completed my program in London, I flew home for my summer internship in the Napa Valley. I lived in a brand new house that my parents had recently built there as a second home and worked from 8am-4pm, Monday through Friday. Since I was living alone at the house, there was no one there to monitor my food intake or behaviors. So, I did whatever I pleased. In the daytime I would work, but in the early mornings and evenings I would eat and run and take laxatives in an attempt to make myself lighter and faster. If running 60 miles a week while taking multiple laxatives a day and attempting to starve yourself isn't abusing your body, I honestly don't know what is.

The habit continued all of the way until I got back to school in the fall to start the fall semester of my junior year. And then everything took a turn for the worst. In the middle of September I severely injured my right plantar fascia (a tendon that runs along the bottom of your foot) and I could no longer run. I could only bike and elliptical. However, biking and using the elliptical just weren't the same as running. I could feel myself getting fatter by the minute. I wanted so badly to weigh less so that I could be thought of as a better coxswain and be selected as one of the 5 out of 10 coxswains on my team to cox a boat at the championship race. That meant I had to be better than at least 5 of them and there was no way I could let my weight be the one thing that held me back after all of the hard work I had been putting in. So naturally, I was upset that one of my quick calorie burning techniques had been taken away. That's when I decided to add throwing up into the mix. I knew that my thoughts and actions surrounding food and exercise were once again becoming extreme as I attempted to purge after almost every meal.

By October, I started having *really* bad days again. When I say really bad days, I am talking about days where I would eat something I considered to be a bad food like a cupcake, and then freak out and then throw it up. To further make up for eating the cupcake, I would wake up, not eat, go for an eight-mile run (on my injured foot), and almost pass out from exhaustion. Or I would eat the cupcake (or other "bad" food), keep it down, but then overdose on 8 or so laxatives to get rid of it. This way was equally as bad though because it ended with me feeling extremely sick the following day and almost passing out in the dorm hallway on the way to the bathroom. Additionally, it would waste almost a day of studying since I would have to call in sick to all of my classes and rowing practice.

I knew it wasn't functional, so I turned myself in to my treatment team to start the recovery process once again. After just one visit with my physician, it was clear that my physical health was getting really bad, once again. My liver numbers were abnormal, my white blood cell count was extremely low from malnutrition, and I had really bad acid reflux. The latter of which was triggered by all of the purging I had been doing.

After speaking with my eating disorder psychologist only three times, she was telling me that I was too sick for her. She didn't think she was qualified enough to treat my condition and its severity and was talking to the rest of my team about referring me out to a more intensive program where they could better help me.

I was desperate to feel better and be free of my eating disorder, but at the same time there was no way I was leaving school or going anywhere. I just wanted to get to Thanksgiving dinner this year and be able to eat it without worrying about how I was going to get rid of it. So despite how tired I was of battling my eating disorder, I typed up an eight week written plan detailing how I was going to stop purging and eat a healthy and balanced diet. I brought "the plan" to my psychologist the following week, who seemed somewhat surprised and told me that she liked my initiative to get better, and if I stuck to this plan I had made, she would delay referring me out. I knew it was going to be hard, but I knew that I needed to do it if I wanted to stay as an outpatient at school. I was overwhelmed by the task at hand, so I spoke with my dietitian at the time about finding a way to maybe take some time off of rowing practice, which was every day, just to focus on my eating. I was worried that this would ruin my chances of being selected for the rowing championship, but at the same time, my dietitian reminded me that if I continued down the path that I was on, I might not be around for spring semester period. So I cleared my schedule, took time away from my rowing practice, and tried to make eating food and not purging a priority.

13

Picking Myself Up Again

The first week of stopping my behaviors was a struggle, but I was lucky that a few of my coxswain friends, whom I was extremely close with, offered me a spot on their couch for the night if I thought I needed extra support. It was harder for me to be in my dorm room alone for fear of binging or purging during the nighttime.

Something that people who have never struggled with an eating disorder may not know is that a lot of anorexics and bulimics will bounce back and forth between the two disorders. I am no exception to this. You see, after I stopped all of the purging behaviors, somewhere in my recovery that winter of my junior year, I slipped back into a restriction pattern and dropped 15 pounds rather quickly. My thought process was something along the lines of: *if I don't overeat I won't feel like I need to get rid of the food.* This thought, however, led me to under-eat, and around the beginning of February I had another dramatic meltdown. I don't remember exactly what happened, but I do remember that it was around 8pm on a Tuesday night. I found myself sobbing on the floor of my room with a giant bottle of Tylenol in one hand about to take them all. I had already swallowed 12 and was contemplating taking the rest. I knew I couldn't tell my friends for fear of freaking them out, so I reached for my phone and called my parents. I told them: "I can't do it anymore. I just can't do it anymore. I hate food and I never want to have to think about food again." Although she couldn't see me on the other end of the line, my mother was about to get on a plane to come get me based on the way I sounded on the phone. I did eventually calm myself down enough to convince her otherwise on the terms that at my next doctor's appointment I would tell my doctor about my thoughts and meltdown. She thought that maybe there was something wrong with a medication in which I had recently had the dosage increased.

I trust my doctors and psychologists, but I was a little bit afraid of sharing all of this with them and I had good reason to be. Telling my doctor the events of my meltdown from just two days before was probably one of the hardest things I ever did. As each word came out of my mouth, I watched her facial expression go from normal to concerned to *oh my god she's lost it*. With the recent weight loss, it just looked really bad. And then came the questions: "Are you still thinking about doing this? Are you going to do it again? Are you sure? Can I trust you not to do anything until I see you next?" I think this was my first time hearing those specific questions, but since then, I've had to answer them many more times because of the way my meltdowns had started to evolve. If you're thinking like that, "call the suicide hotline, call 911 or go to the ER" is what any medical professional will tell you. Of course you never actually use any of those options because in your mind you're not sick enough and that's only for people who are actually sick.

That particular time, I of course said no to all of the questions, but I was bumped up to weekly visits for the next few weeks instead of every 2 weeks, since I was now a high-risk patient.

I remember when I left that day, my doctor looked me in the eye and said: "You know you can't live off of yogurt and berries forever. Please don't restrict this week. Your body is already under stress and you're going to start fainting soon." I said "ok" and carried on.

I didn't make the spring training trip to Tennessee and I'm 99.9% sure it was because of my weight. I was one of only two coxswains that didn't make the trip and some of the coxswains who did make the trip weren't as experienced or seasoned as I was.

The Tuesday morning before the spring training trip announcement went out, the coaches decided to take everybody's weight at practice. I wasn't at practice that morning because of an accounting exam I had to attend to. Later that day I got an email from the team's sports nutritionist saying that my coach "needed my weight before he could make spring break decisions." She didn't want to weigh me though. She knew I would flip out and it would make me not trust her anymore, so instead she had me come in on a Friday morning during one of the rower's lifting sessions to get weighed by the strength coach.

I remember weighing the lightest I ever had that morning. I wasn't sure if it was good or bad, it's just what I was at that point. I was pretty sure it was because I had stopped the binge/purge cycle over the winter and somehow had transitioned to eating not enough. Two days later, when the spring training trip list came out, I wasn't on it. Needless to say, I was devastated. Some of my friends on the rowing team were sad for me too. They didn't understand why the coaches didn't select me to go and neither did I, so I came to the conclusion that I was too light and that they didn't want to encourage my anorexia.

Simultaneously though, that incident led me to develop a newly found trust in my teammates that I didn't have before. Many of them sent me messages or spoke to me after the spring break list had come out expressing their regret of me not being selected for the trip and that they were sorry it happened. They backed up their expressions by telling me that I was better and more experienced than a few of the girls who had been selected to cox on spring break, so they weren't sure why I was left behind. For the first time ever, I could see that they were there for me and that they weren't going to leave me or stop being friends with me just because I wasn't going on the trip with them. I focused on my recovery and growing my friendships for the remainder of my junior year and saw it open some new doors for me. I even watched myself get better at coxing because there was so much more free space in my mind. I wasn't preoccupied with what other people thought of me and could focus better from the consistent flow of energy I was getting from food.

With the support of my teammates, I was selected to cox an eight at the championship. It felt amazing to be wanted for my skill and hard work that I had put into the sport of rowing over the previous three years. It was especially an honor for me to be one of the few selected coxswains. Being in a set championship boat also enabled me to become closer with the eight other girls I got to work with leading up to the race. I knew that each of the girls depended on me for their own performance, so getting to know them was helpful in fostering a connection of trust and understanding between us so that we could work together well during the race. As a result, my friendships with these girls blossomed. I even developed a special connection with a girl in my boat, Laila, whom I grew to love for her caring nature and passion for rowing.

The following summer, between my junior and senior year of college, my friendship with Laila grew stronger since she and I had both stayed for summer school on campus for six weeks. There were a few other girls on the team who had also stayed for summer school. All of us got together and went out many times. Prior to that summer I hadn't gone out much because of the stress and anxiety those situations

typically cause me. I really enjoyed it though and I remember feeling

more included that summer than I had in a long time. I was finally

reaching the level of emotional connectivity and friendship that any

neurotypical[3] girl would experience. It felt really good. I was also

looking forward to living with one of these teammates the coming fall.

---

[3] Neurotypical is a word that many people with Asperger Syndrome and Autism
Spectrum Disorder use to describe those who don't have it.

14

So Done

It's funny how all of my college years seem to blur together in terms of my eating disorder. The cycle of ups and downs did not stop once I had quit purging and taking laxatives. The aftermath involved numerous trips to doctors' offices and hospitals to fix my body that was ravaged by abnormal stress levels and malnutrition.

The truth is that even if there is physical recovery from anorexia, the anorexic mindset is *so hard* to eradicate since the composition of your brain has changed. Perhaps that is the reason why anorexia has the highest mortality rate of any psychiatric illness. Looking back, I can see that I was slowly killing myself, and I could not control it. I would not wish that experience on anyone. I feel so blessed to have the support I needed to recover, to fight anorexia. In treatment, I learned that anorexia has a biological component that is hard to control once you are sick. I also learned that anorexia has a tendency to show its presence during times of high stress. As a student and Division 1 athlete at a prestigious university, there were ample opportunities for stress to manifest itself in my daily life.

The fall semester of my senior year turned out to be a stress-filled disaster. The stressors came at me from all angles. I was in a fight with my parents. I was tackling grad school applications and spending long days trying to maintain my performance in school and rowing. To top all of that off, I was overwhelmed living in a house with five other girls. Something needed to change; I could not sustain this lifestyle.

Even though I was attending parties and going to bars with friends like any other girl my age, my stress was becoming unmanageable. And it definitely didn't help when some memories of my Morgan High days resurfaced upon an email I received regarding the death of a girl who was in the mother-daughter group I had been a part of for six years growing up. It wasn't so much that she had died of a heroin overdose that upset me as it was that it sparked a few conversations with Dr. Mallory that reminded me of my high school days again. It still pained me to remember how people had treated me back then. So I naturally reached out for anorexia's hand in hopes that it would soothe my unsettling feelings.

My friends and teammates could see that I was slipping and they wanted to help, but they didn't know how. As I got sicker, my suicidal thoughts returned and became stronger with each passing day.

I thought I could combat them though, at least until Thanksgiving when I would get a nice break at home to focus only eating. At least that's what I told myself anyway. I was so close too, but not close enough.

The breakdown happened the Thursday afternoon before Thanksgiving break. It started at rowing practice. The team was inside that day in the erg room[4] since it was too cold to row outside on the river. During the cold weather, we had many practices indoors, so this wasn't uncommon. It had been just like any other normal indoor practice. The rowers erged for 60 or 70 minutes while I sat on one of the spin bikes in the back and got my own workout in.

---

[4] An erg room is a large room with about 60 ergs (rowing machines) that a rowing team uses to practice on when they aren't on the water in boats.

As practice was ending, my coach called me into the conference room. Not knowing the full extent of my situation, he expressed his concern that I was moving out of my teammate's house without telling her. I was at the end of my rope. I didn't want to have to explain myself because I just couldn't deal with it. So I stormed out of his office.

I was so upset and angry. I immediately went to the locker room where my teammates were showering and cleaning up for dinner, approaching my teammate whose house I had been living in. I told her I was leaving her house, then angrily typed up an email to my coach, informing him that she now knew. I was in complete sensory overload and left the locker room crying hysterically. Too much was happening at once.

I got in the car and called my friend sobbing and told her what I had done. A good friend and teammate of mine, she insisted that I make things right with our coach first and apologize to him for the email that I had angrily sent from the locker room. Since I was no longer staying in my teammate's house, I drove to the hotel my parents had gotten for me to stay in. It was only upon pulling into the parking lot there that I saw I had a new phone message. It was from my coach. Being the kind person that he is, he had left a message saying that he was sorry that I was upset about our earlier conversation and wanted to try and work it out. I was sorry too, so I sent him an apology email from my laptop.

However my emotions still had yet to run their course. Life was falling apart at the seams and I couldn't hold it together. I just needed someone to hold me and tell me it was ok. That everything would be fine. So I put a post up on my eating disorder recovery Instagram account I had created about a year prior when I finally decided to commit to recovery. A black one that detailed my current frame of mind and the thoughts I had.

Not too long after I put the post up I realized that I had left my makeup bag in the locker room at school and needed to drive back to get it so that I could shower. So I got in the car to go back to campus to get it. My friends who followed me then on my recovery account saw the post and had asked me about it so I took it down and told them I was fine. I was starting to calm down. I called my mom and after talking with her for a bit, I decided I was going to play the piano on campus, one of my coping strategies I had developed, and then take a hot shower back at my hotel and go to sleep. Then I would start over the next day and try to make things right.

Laila, who was now a close friend of mine, had seen the Instagram post before I deleted it and asked me if I could meet her on campus to talk about it. I told her I was returning to campus to get my bag I had left in the locker room, and asked her to meet me there. Laila wasn't the only one who met me there though. It turns out that she had sent the Instagram post to one of my rowing coaches, who was also there waiting for me. Before I knew it, I was dragged out of the rowing locker room kicking and screaming by two police officers to the medical center on my campus where I was detained for three hours. The police officers were brutal and grabbed my flailing arms despite my effort to cooperate, telling them that I would comply with their request and walk myself to the center. If you're familiar with autism, you might know that you should never touch an autistic person in the middle of a meltdown who doesn't want to be touched. After all, I was already experiencing sensory overload, and that made it 1000 times worse.

When asked, I denied everything about my Instagram post. I didn't think it was fair that I was being held captive for it since it had already been deleted. I tried to stay quiet, in control, and answer the psychologist's questions according to what my mom texted me to say. She was trying her best to keep me calm since she knew I was having a meltdown. She knew that, if I acted out, they wouldn't understand and would continue to treat me with disrespect or worse… drug me. So I tried my best to hold it together while my mom convinced the on-call psychologist to let me out over the phone.

They did eventually release me, though I was petrified. I had been pushed around, taken against my will, grabbed, and almost sedated. What could be more frightening to a twenty-one year old girl?

As soon as I got out of the detainment at the medical center, my parents were quick to book me a flight home. They had already called Dr. Mallory, who was in the process of getting me a temporary medical leave from classes. Maybe that's what I needed. I wasn't eating and was now traumatized and unable to calm myself down enough to sleep.

By the time I arrived home the following day, I hadn't slept since the night before the incident. So I slept while my mom cooked for me to try and get me nourished enough to think straight again.

"It's just a setback," she would say… "Your life isn't going to fall apart again. You're going to be ok. You just need to eat."

15

Creating My Future

I think that was the final indicator to my family and friends of just how bad my struggle was. I didn't want to uproot my life completely and forgo the work I had put into my final semester and to rowing, so I chose to continue to work with my medical team on an outpatient basis. After the fall's drama, everyone seemed to be skeptical of me. Despite my doctor's permission to return to school, some of my teammates treated me differently than they had before the incident because they didn't think I was well enough to be at school and were upset by the drama I had caused. Some of them stopped responding to my texts, liking my Instagram posts, and talking to me. It was like they had cut *i* from their world. Among them was my good friend, Laila, who had met me in the locker room the night of the detainment. She had been there to watch as I was grabbed and dragged out of the athletic complex by the police. I think that's what killed me the most following the incident; Losing her friendship.

As if that wasn't enough, a few teammates even went as far as to display their distaste for my behavior by giving me bad coxswain evaluations the following spring, so that I wouldn't be in their boat. When I asked them directly why they were treating me differently than they had in the past, they told me they didn't want to get close to me because if any more drama occurred they didn't want to be involved or know about it. While I was definitely sad and hurt that some of my teammates were treating me this way, my close friends and I knew it was because they didn't understand. After all, Dr. Mallory, my parents, and I had agreed on a plan. I knew I didn't want to spend any more of my life living with anorexia, so I was going to spend the summer getting better no matter what it would take to get there. There was going to be no more messing around. I would be going to a teaching hospital for an evidence-based treatment I had yet to try. I was already on the list to see a doctor at the Eating Disorders Program at the University of

California San Francisco. I would start treatment there the week after graduation. No summer internship or travels, just anorexia treatment.

In the interim, I knew I needed to maintain my composure and fly under the radar so that I could finish my last rowing season and graduate. My parents, Dr. Mallory, and I knew it was best not to interrupt my last semester of college because they wanted me to be able to spend it with the friends that I loved. My dorm friends had proved to be the ones who stuck by me despite all of my challenges and I was glad to spend the rest of my senior year hanging out with them. So I spent most of the spring laying low, focusing on my classes, and making the best out of my last rowing season. Of course, I was dead set on going to the championship again and finishing my collegiate rowing career strong.

In March, I was accepted to my top choice graduate program, Columbia University. It's funny because, before my freshman year of high school, attending an Ivy League college had been my dream. However, I had given up on that dream after my experience at the Anna Feld School where I had been discriminated against and called an Asian hater. There was just no way I could want that after everything that happened there. Now here it was, almost eight years later, and that long lost dream was about to become a reality for me. I was beginning to feel a sense of excitement for my new future.

My last spring at university wasn't without its hiccups though. In April, I surprisingly didn't make the coxswain cut for the California trip. I was told by some teammates that one of the rowers in the boat I was supposed to cox had rallied to get me booted out on the last minute coxswain evaluation that had been sent out. Despite the setback, I was still able to get a boat for the championship. To further boost my ego, I was in what most would consider to be a higher priority boat than the one that went to California anyway. At the championship, I coxed two of the best races of my career. I remember listening to my tape after and actually thinking, *wow… I nailed it.* I didn't care much that my team hadn't placed as well as they had hoped to, because I was proud of my personal performance and I knew I had finished strong and improved. I was ready to continue my career and move up to the next level as a coxswain. It definitely didn't feel like the end of my career at that race, but more just the beginning of a new chapter.

Also, that week was my last medical visit at school before my care was transferred to UCSF. The visit was bittersweet. I remember my nurse looked at me and said: "You're going to have a really good life." Tears filled my eyes as I walked away. She had been through two and a half years of my eating disorder with me and I knew that now it was up to me to really commit to getting better and stopping my obsession with food. I wanted to be able to come back some day in the future and tell them that I had finally recovered.

On graduation morning, I walked around the lawn outside of the stadium with one of my best friends as we waited to line up and walk into our graduation ceremony. It was freezing cold that day, but I was glad at how different that day was for me than the one when I graduated from high school just four years earlier. I had someone to sit with and to talk to. I was graduating with a group of girls who never left my side from day one. The girls who I ate with at the dining hall, who taught me the school fight song, and whose rooms I spent countless hours in, procrastinating on schoolwork.

Finally, after the ceremonies were over, my friends and I waited in the long line to take photos on the sacred main building steps. It would be the last two hours we all spent together at the place that had been our home for the last four years. Per university tradition, we had waited four years to even be allowed to climb those steps and throw our hats up in the air. When we got to the front of the line, the feeling

of running up the stairs together for the first time was incredible and is

something I will remember forever. I have never felt such a strong

connection to a place and to people as I did during my years at

university.

16

A Million Miles Later

Although this is where my story ends, I know I am still growing and changing each and every day. There will be times when I struggle with who I am, but I know it is the shoes I had to walk in that have made me stronger and better able to handle life's challenges. I know there are many things that even my closest friends will never be able to understand. Like how much it means to me when they send me a text message, get a meal with me, or just hang out. Or even when people I know say hi to me. It's all of these small acts of kindness that most people take for granted, that I didn't have for a long time.

I know now that making friends and socializing does not come naturally to me. It is something that I have had to learn and practice.

My past experiences will always be with me in the back of my mind. They are ingrained in my memory and always will be. These experiences have made me the person I am today.

Acknowledgements

First and foremost, I want to thank my family. My family has been my grounding framework in life and has stayed by me through every up and down I have experienced.

I also want to thank the friends I made at university for their encouragement of me writing this book. I wouldn't have been able to do this without you. I remember when I wrote my very first chapter and read it out loud one night in the dorm three and a half years ago. The silence that took over the room with each spoken word was incredible. It was the reading of that chapter and the response I received that inspired me to complete the project.

Thank you to all of my editors for taking the time to help me come out with the most poised and polished memoir that I possibly could. You are all incredible and offered great ideas and insight.

A huge thank you goes to my long time child-adolescent psychologist. My achievements and social successes wouldn't have been possible without your support.

Finally, I would like to thank all of my doctors over the years. A huge thank you goes to my team, who helped me recover from

Anorexia Nervosa, and to my doctor who formally diagnosed me with an Autism Spectrum Disorder.

Printed in the USA
CPSIA information can be obtained
at www.ICGtesting.com
LVHW090152010524
779006LV00005B/78